MW00607022

The Divine Activation of Faith

The Divine Activation of Faith and the Myth of Free Will

Clyde L. Pilkington, Jr.

BIBLE STUDENT'S PRESS™
Windber, Pennsylvania

The Divine Activation of Faith and the Myth of Free Will
by Clyde L. Pilkington, Jr.
Copyright © 2019 by Clyde L. Pilkington, Jr.
All rights reserved.

Originally printing:
   Individual articles published in the Bible Student's Notebook, ©1989-2018

Second Printing:
   First book edition, 2019

Executive Editor: André Sneidar
Layout and Design: Great Adventure in Faith

Cover design by Nathan Hyde Pilkington

         Paperback ISBN: 978-1-62904-328-9
         Hardback ISBN: 978-1-62904-327-2

Published by:
   Bible Student's Press™
   An imprint of *Pilkington & Sons*
   P.O. Box 265
   Windber, PA 15963
   1-800-784-6010

For information on *Bible Student's Press*™ releases, visit
   www.BibleStudentsPress.com

For information on other Bible study resources, visit
   www.StudyShelf.com

Printed in the United States of America.

CONTENTS

Chapter 1
Faith: What is it?

So then faith cometh by hearing, and hearing by the Word of God (Romans 10:17).

For many, faith is actually human presumption or religious superstition. However, faith is simply taking God at His word. Look at the great example of Abraham, Israel's father of faith.

Abraham believed God, and it was counted unto him for righteousness (Romans 4:3).

This passage tells us that Abraham believed *"believed God."* That is, he believed what God *said!*

Noah Webster defined "faith" as,

> the assent (or agreement) of the mind to the truth of what is declared by another, resting on his authority and veracity [habitual truthfulness], without evidence; The judgment that what another states or testifies is the truth.[1]

Faith is simply *believing God;* it is taking Him at His Word. In other words faith requires a declaration from God to exist. Thus, God's Word is the very foundation of faith:

So then faith cometh by hearing, and hearing by the Word of God (Romans 10:17).

There can be no faith until God has made a declaration. One cannot assume or presume upon the declarations of God. The declarations

---

1. *The American Dictionary of the English Language* (1828).

must actually be the words of God.[2] There is no other means! One must "hear" the Word of God. The enticing words of man's wisdom will not do![3]

Now, take special notice of the connection between faith and the hearing of God's Word.

> *In Whom you also trusted, **after** that ye heard the Word of Truth, the gospel of your salvation* (Ephesians 1:13).

Faith, based then on the Word of God, is not human imagination or religious mythology. It is merely a dependence, a resting on the declarations of God.

Going back to Abraham, we see that he believed the specific declarations that God made concerning him.

> *And, behold, the word of the* LORD *came unto him, saying,*
>   *"This shall not be your heir; but he that shall come forth out of your own bowels shall be your heir."*
> *And He brought him forth abroad, and said,*
>   *"Look now toward Heaven, and count the stars, if you be able to number them."*
> *And He said unto him,*
>   *"So shall your seed be."*
> *And he believed in the* LORD; *and He counted it to him for righteousness* (Genesis 15:4-6).

The "good news" to Abraham was, *"So shall your seed be."* This was the declaration of God *to him.* This was the *"gospel"* of his salvation – the means of his justification. Thus, Paul speaks to us of *"the gospel*

---

2. "There are far too many who think that faith is a long lever that we can use to pry things out of God. It is believed that if a man can lay hold of that mysterious thing called 'faith' that he can get God to bless with success every wild scheme and project that he sets out to accomplish. When they fail they usually whimper the childish excuse that they did not have faith enough, implying that if they had worked up a little more faith they would have succeeded." – Otis Q. Sellers (1901-1992), Seed & Bread, #109.
3. I Corinthians 2:4-5; *cf.* 1:18, 24; Romans 1:16.

of your salvation" (Ephesians 1:13), which was unique to the revelation committed to him – which Paul termed *"my gospel."*[4]

Thus, we see the importance of understanding the declarations of God *to us*. While all of God's words are *for us*, they certainly are not all *to us*, or concerning *us*.

---

4. Romans 2:16; 16:25; II Timothy 2:8.

Chapter 2
Faith: The Gift of God

For by grace are you saved through faith; and that not of yourselves: it is the gift of God (Ephesians 2:8).

All Things Are of God

God is the Sovereign Originator, Placer and Subjector,[1] thus all things come from His hand. Faith is no exception.

> *For of Him, and through Him, and to Him, are all things* (Romans 11:36).

God brought "*all things*" into existence and placed them where they are, and has subjected them to the conditions and circumstances in which they find themselves. "*All things*" have their course in God. He is behind all of the circumstances and movements of His creation. "All" is out of God, through God, and to Him.

> *… He does according to His will in the army of heaven, and among the inhabitants of the earth: and none can stay His hand, or say to Him, "What are You doing?"* (Daniel 4:35).

> *In Whom also we have obtained an inheritance, being predestinated according to the purpose of Him Who works all things after the counsel of His Own will* (Ephesians 1:11).

---

1. Originator, Placer and Subjector are the meaning of the words translated "*God.*" The bacis Hebrew words for "God" are *Elohim* (meaning "*Originator*") and *El* (meaning "*Subjector*"), while the Greek word is *Theos* (meaning "*Placer*").

God Is the Source of Faith in Believers

Since absolutely *"all"* is out of God, through God, and to Him, faith then is certainly no exception.

> *For it is given to you in the behalf of Christ, not only to believe on Him, but also to suffer for His sake* (Philippians 1:29).

> *For I say, through the grace given to me, to every man who is among you, not to think of himself more highly than he ought to think; but to think soberly, according as God has dealt to every man the measure of faith* (Romans 12:3).

> *For by grace are you saved through faith; and that not of yourselves: it is the gift of God: not of works, lest any man should boast* (Ephesians 2:8-9).

God Is the Source of the Current Unbelief in Unbelievers

Conversely then, even unbelief clearly comes from God's hand as well.

> *Therefore has He mercy on whom He will have mercy, and whom He will He hardens* (Romans 9:18).

> *God has given them the spirit of slumber, eyes that they should not see, and ears that they should not hear* (Romans 11:8).

> *For God has concluded them all in unbelief, that He might have mercy on all* (Romans 11:32).

God Will Be the Source of Faith in All

Don't be discouraged as you look around you. What you see is not the end of God's plan and purpose. Granted, the world is filled with sin and unbelief; but God is not yet done. Don't judge the final outcome by the current state of things. This is not the finished product of God. Those of us who now trust the Lord Jesus Christ are but the beginning of God's glorious work.

The current state of things is not the way that they will always be. Those who believe during their lifetime are "*a kind of firstfruits of His creatures*" (James 1:18). These "*firstfruits*" are the divine guarantee of a full harvest. None will be left out, for God will one day be the source of faith to all.

> *According as God has dealt to every man the measure of faith* (Romans 12:3).

> *... He has given faith to all men ...* (Acts 17:31).

> *That at the name of Jesus every knee should bow ... And that every tongue should confess that Jesus Christ is Lord, to the glory of God the Father* (Philippians 2:10-11).

> *No man can say that Jesus is the Lord, but by the Holy Spirit* (I Corinthians 12:3).

Chapter 3

Firstfruits

In every harvest there is that small portion of the crop that ma-
tures early, before the vast majority of the rest. These are called
"firstfruits." They are a token of that which is to come – the full
harvest.

Under the Old Testament economy the *"firstfruits"* belonged especially to God, and were holy to Him. In every generation, and in every place, God has had His *"firstfruits"* – those that come to harvest
earlier than the rest.

> *My well-beloved Epaenetus, who is the **firstfruits** of Achaia
> unto Christ* (Romans 16:5).

> *Of His own will begat He us with the word of truth, that we
> should be a kind of **firstfruits** of His creatures* (James 1:18).

> *These were redeemed from among men, being the **firstfruits**
> unto God and to the Lamb* (Revelation 14:4).

These *"firstfruits"* are those who have been selected by God to believe early. They are His "called-ones," or "called-out-ones" – the
ecclesia.[1] This calling is to a place of divine service. Those who have

---

1. Ecclesia (ἐκκλησία) is the Greek word commonly translated as "church" in most
   English versions. It is a compound word meaning "called-out" (*ek* = "out"; *kaleō*
   = "called"). The ecclesia is God's "called-out" ones. The ecclesia is not a building

been selected early to believe will fulfill an important role in bringing in the rest of God's harvest.

---

or denomination; not a meeting, or doctrinal creed; it is not somewhere we go, or something we do, it is who we as believers *are*. For more information see the author's book, *The Outsiders*.

Chapter 4
Tɧe Calleɓ

Among whom are you also the calleɓ of Je-
sus Chriѕte gift of Goɓ (Romans 1:6).

Those of us who have trusted the Lord Jesus Christ, and are now saved by His grace, did not do so by chance. It was all a part of the divine plan.

*He has **chosen us** in Him **before** the disruption of the world* (Ephesians 1:4).

It was God who gave us our faith to believe and respond to His calling. The calling of God is an *"election"* to divine service:

*Knowing, brethren beloved, **your election** of God* (I Thessalonians 1:4).

*For the children being not yet born, neither having done any good or evil, that the purpose of God according to **election** might stand, not of works, but of Him that **calls*** (Romans 9:11).

God has not *"saved us, and called us with a holy calling"* simply to abandon the rest of mankind in eternal torment. We are but the *beginning stage* of Christ's redemptive work. God's ultimate plan includes *all* of His creation. None will be permanently lost.[1]

God currently seeks neither to reveal Himself nor His plan to the masses. If it was His purpose, He would have accomplished it long

---

1.   See the author's work *Nothing Will Be Lost*.

ago. The fact is that He has taken elaborate steps to assure that He and His plan are sufficiently hidden from the masses.

> *You have **hid** these things from the wise and prudent, and hast revealed them unto babes* (Matthew 11:25).

> *But they understood not this saying, and it was **hid** from them, that they perceived it not* (Luke 9:45).

Instead, God chooses who He wants to receive His revelation *at this time:*

> *All men cannot receive this saying, except those to whom it is given* (Matthew 19:11).

God's plan on the stage of human history initially is to reveal Himself to a few – the *"remnant,"* the *"called,"* the *"elect."* This is why our salvation and calling is *"according to His Own purpose and grace,"* both of which were given to us *"before times eonian."*

> *Who hath saved us, and **called** us with an holy calling, not according to our works, but according to His own purpose and grace, which was given us in Christ Jesus before times eonian* (II Timothy 1:9).

God draws those whom He has *chosen*, whether in His past dealings with Israel, or His present dealings with the members of the Body of Christ.

THE BODY OF CHRIST

> *According as He has **chosen** us in Him before the disruption of the world, that we should be holy and without blame before Him in love* (Ephesians 1:4).

God's calling has always been to a few. He told Israel that He did not set His love upon them, nor choose them, because they were more in number than any people, but because they were *"the fewest of all people"* (Deuteronomy 7:7).

God's calling also has always been to service. The reason that God has called only a few during the course of human history is that He is calling out a *small* company of servants for His name.

God has called a few whom He is preparing to rule with Him, *serving* the rest of creation.

A survey through the Scripture's use of the word *"chosen"* will reveal that God's calling is one to service:

> *God has **chosen** him ... to stand **to minister** in the name of the LORD* (Deuteronomy 18:5).

> *... them the LORD thy God has **chosen to minister** unto Him* (Deuteronomy 21:5).

> *... them has the LORD **chosen** ... **to minister** unto Him ...* (I Chronicles 15:2).

> *the LORD has **chosen you** ... **to serve** Him, and that you should **minister** unto Him* (II Chronicles 29:11).

Now notice Isaiah 43:10, for it is of particular significance as to one's calling in relationship to God Himself:

> *My servant whom I have chosen: that you may know and believe Me, and understand that I am He.*

God draws His *chosen* into personal relationship with Himself. He has chosen us for the purpose of *knowing* Him, *believing* Him and *understanding* Him. *This* is our calling.

The religious are satisfied to learn *about* Him, the chosen are given the heart for actually *knowing Him*. Paul wrote,

That I may KNOW *Him, and the power of His resurrection, and the fellowship of His sufferings, being made conformable unto His death* (Philippians 3:10).

Man's religious systems blind and bind men, sidetracking them by endless busy-work – meetings, group activities, projects and mass instruction, all resulting in a secondhand "knowledge" and "faith" concerning "God."

Our particular culture's religious masses are "Christian"; but if they lived in another culture they undoubtedly would have adapted the context of its religious persuasion (*e.g.* Islam, Buddhism, etc.).

God is now tutoring *"the Called"* for service in the *"heavenly places."* We are a part of the Many-Membered Christ, the Firstborn.

We are called by Paul's Gospel,[2] into a "not many,"[3] divine vocation,[4] that is a High,[5] Holy[6] calling, predestinated,[7]

before the disruption of the world.[8]

Our Calling was *from the Beginning:*

... God hath from the beginning chosen you ... (II Thessalonians 2:13).

How truly humbling all of this should be to us.

For by grace are ye saved through faith; and that not of yourselves: it is the gift of God: not of works, lest any man should boast (Romans 2:8-9).

---

2. *"He called you by our gospel"* (II Thessalonians 2:14).
3. *"... Not many wise men after the flesh, not many mighty, not many noble, are called"* (I Corinthians 1:26).
4. *"... The vocation wherewith ye are called"* (Ephesians 4:1).
5. *"... The high calling of God in Christ Jesus"* (Philippians 3:14).
6. *"... Called us with an holy calling ..."* (II Timothy 1:9).
7. *"... Whom He did predestinate, them He also called ..."* (Romans 8:30).
8. Ephesians 1:4.

Chapter 3
Divine Activation

Recently a new debit card came in the mail from the bank. It had a sticker on it that stated "Activation Required." Until this necessary activation took place, for all intents and purposes, this card was like any other piece of plastic. However, once it was activated, it took on a meaning and purpose quite distinct from other plastics. It was activated to begin its specifically designed purpose. The card was then ready for use in its predetermined function.

So it is with the believer; there comes a time when God "activates" those whom He has called. He grants them faith: the eyes to see and the ears to hear. This activation sets in motion a progression of divine utilization. God cultivates in the believer a responsive relationship – one of intimate, conscious participation in the divine will, decree and course – not limited to His direction and control of the ages, but in the details of our lives and those with whom we interact as well. Believers become more and more aware of His hand in everything, and that they are channels of His life.

For example, by realization and growth in and of Him, even our first conscious thoughts in the morning can progress to be,

> Good morning Dad. I'm thankful that I know You – Who you really are – and that I know who I am. I am eager to see what you have written for me today. I am thankful that you have granted me the awareness of your active direction and control of all things, including me and this day. My heart's desire is to live keenly in that awareness today, as your willing servant, as well as your faithful son."

Concerning our divine beginning and progression, Paul wonderfully writes,

> *Being confident of this very thing, that He Who began a good work in you will perform it until the day of Jesus Christ"* (Philippians 1:6).

Chapter 4
The Nature of Faith

Is It Really "All or Nothing"?

There are those who would make faith "all or nothing." Among those who do there are a wide range of doctrinal and/or behavioral requirements for one to be a believer. Many of their criteria create domino effects that can be far reaching, if not seemingly limitless.

I grew up in the depth of the religious system. Most of my denominational life I heard, "You can't possibly be a believer if ..." What would follow, depending on exactly who you talked with, would be a host of doctrines and practices that either were mandatory or prohibitive in order to be a believer. Each sect exalts their own understandings of Scripture as *the standard* for what true "faith" is. If you miss a single one of the "essential" tenets of *their* "faith," you are labeled as an "unbeliever."

Is Faith "All or Nothing"?

Some evidently have difficulty in grasping the mixture of faith with unbelief, because they mistakenly see belief as "all or nothing." No such concept of faith originates from Scripture, but from the supposed superiority of manmade reasoning and religious standards. The simple fact is that, because of the very nature of faith, those who believe may, and often do, also experience areas or degrees of unbelief.

THE SIMPLICITY OF FAITH

The book of Mark records a father who by simple faith brought his tormented son to our Lord.

Consider his heartfelt cry,

> Lord, I believe; help my unbelief (9:24)

Or as Rotherham renders it,

> I have faith! Help my want [i.e., lack] of faith.

Who, reading this, has not at some point identified with the force and passion of these heartfelt words?

A MEASURE OF FAITH

Having a mixture of faith and unbelief at the same time is possible because, as Paul made plain, faith – instead of being all or nothing – is actually granted in *"measures."*

> … unto each one, God has dealt a measure of faith (Romans 12:3).[1]

To use terms we can all identify with – around the house we may have measures of a teaspoon (or smaller), and on the other end of the scale, that of a 5-gallon bucket (or larger). These are quite different, unequal measures – but both are genuine measures nonetheless. Thus, our Lord's striking illustration concerning a small measure of the kingdom-faith as being like that of a mustard seed (Matthew 17:20).

Not only that, but to put it another way, Paul also speaks of those who are *"strong,"* as well as those who are *"weak"* in faith (Romans

---

1. *"A measure of faith"* (Rotherham; Young; Green); *"faithing"* (Dabhar).

14)[2], even as Scripture speaks of *"great faith"*[3] and *"little faith."*[4] Nonetheless, Paul did not discount those who had a small or weak measure of faith as being "faithless" nor "unbelievers."

Even our Lord's own chosen apostles petitioned Him for an *increased* measure of faith.

> *The apostles said unto the Lord, "Increase our faith!"* (Luke 17:5).

Paul, speaking to the saints at Thessalonica, said of them,

> *... your faith grows exceedingly* (II Thessalonian 1:3).

Now, apply this nature of faith to the most basic elements of Paul's gospel: the death, burial and resurrection of Christ. What would a small and weak measure of faith look like in regards to these foundational truths? Likewise, what would a great and strong measure of faith look like? How could we apply an *increase* and *growth* of faith concerning the death, burial and resurrection? The mistaken theology of some would not make allowance for such growth.

FAITH'S INFANCY

Just as individuals progress from infancy to maturity, so it is with the life of faith. Just because one is immature mentally and/or physically does not mean that they are not yet an individual. Likewise, just because one has an infant or immature form of faith does not mean that they are therefore an unbeliever.

The most basic form of faith is to be found in simply believing that *"God is."* This constitutes faith's first approach toward God.

> *Without faith it is impossible to please Him: for he who comes to God **must believe that He is,** and that He is a rewarder of*

---

2. Cf. "strong in faith" (Romans 4:20); "weak in faith" (:19).
3. Matthew 8:10; 15:28; Luke 7:9.
4. Matthew 6:30; 8:26; 14:31; 16:8; 17:20; Luke 12:28.

those who diligently seek Him (Hebrews 11:6).

The Way of God More Perfectly

In the Book of Acts we have a wonderful example of Apollos being helped along on his journey of faith by Aquila and Priscilla. He knew only the baptism of John and was shown *"the way of God more perfectly"* by them (18:24-26). This is the nature of our ministry toward others of faith – a work toward perfection, or maturity of faith.

Our Attitude and Approach Toward Those with Weak Faith

What is Paul's instruction concerning those who are weak in faith? One simple word: *Reception.*

> *Him that is weak in his faith, receive ...* (Romans 14:1, Rotherham).

Paul did not diminish as "faithless" or "unbelievers" those who had a small or weak measure of faith. Quite the contrary, they were to be *received* (:1), and that reception was in the same way that we ourselves have been received by Christ (15:7). Paul also stressed that this reception was not to be for the purpose of belittling and debating their weak faith. Notice the rest of Romans 14:1.

not to doubtful disputations (KJV)

not for discrimination of reasonings (CV)

not to determinations of reasonings (Young)

not for differences of reasoning (Diaglott)

not for disputing opinions (Rotherham)

So, Just Who Is a Believer?

So, some will pose the question as to who is a believer. The answer is really quite simple. Believers are those whom God has called. We are not believers *because* we believe; we believe because we are called of God and granted a measure of faith to believe – however small or weak that faith may be. Faith is entirely the operation of the self-revealing God.

While some religious leaders will take it upon themselves to decide who is or is not a believer, Paul, at the end of his ministry, was quite content to leave the answer of who belonged to our Lord *with our Lord Himself.*

Nevertheless the foundation of God stands sure, having this seal, **The Lord knows them who are His** (II Timothy 2:19).

Chapter 7
Unbelieving Believers

Therefore, I also, on hearing of this faith of yours in the Lord Jesus, and that for all the saints, do not cease giving thanks for you, making mention in my prayers, that the God of our Lord Jesus Christ, the Father of glory, may be giving you a spirit of wisdom and revelation in the realization of Him (Ephesians 1:15-17, Concordant).

While belief and unbelief are contrasting opposites, they can be and are present at the same time in all of us. We are all unbelieving believers to some degree: "*I believe! Help my unbelief!*" (Mark 9:24). In fact, the purpose of teaching believers is to help their unbelief. It is to build them up in faith.[1]

Even between believers who are most closely aligned doctrinally with each other, there are often many subjects about which they might hold differing opinions. On every one of these subjects *at least* one of these believers does not believe the truth of Scriptures: they are unbelieving believers on that particular subject.

"*Realization*" is a grand truth, but it is progressive. Paul distinguishes the progression of "*realization*" from the initial "*believing*" of faith. This is why Paul prayed for "*the saints*" (Ephesians 1:1, 15-16), who had already heard the "*gospel*" of their salvation and believed on

---

1. "*Edify*" is the translation of the Greek word οἰκοδομή (*oikodomē*), the word for "*architecture*, that is, a *structure*" (Strong), thus it is "the act of building, building up" (Thayer).

Christ (:13). His prayer for them was that God would give these believers a *"realization"* (:17, *"knowledge,"* KJV), *i.e.,* that they may *"attain ... realization"* (4:13). Thus, there are surely believers who had not yet been granted *"realization":* they were unbelieving believers.

Of what was Paul praying that these believers would have a *"realization"*? Of God and His Son: *"the realization of Him"* (1:17), *"the realization of the Son of God"* (4:13).

Thus the believers to whom Paul wrote, just as with the believers of our day, lacked a most basic *"realization"* of even God and His Son. None of us are granted *"all faith"* upon believing. This realization is progressive; a journey that we'll be on for the duration of our lives. The understanding of God and His Son, while our most basic foundation, as it turns out, is also the deepest of revelations.

We must not confuse the initial beginning of faith with the process of realization.

I believe! Help my unbelief! (Mark 9:24).

Chapter 6
Faith and the Unbeliever

Christendom has made death the end of God's grace and mercy.

Yet God will bring His entire creation to the place of faith, in His *Own* good time and way. All eventually will be brought to belief by their Creator, although not all in *this* lifetime. Not all will be saved by pure "faith" – it will take "sight" for some to believe. Two great examples of this readily come to mind. "Doubting Thomas" was one.

Thomas

> *The other disciples therefore said to him, "We have seen the Lord." But he said to them, "Except I shall see in His hands the print of the nails, and put my finger into the print of the nails, and thrust my hand into His side, I will not believe"* (John 20:25).

To which Jesus Christ responded:

> *Then He said to Thomas, "Reach here your finger, and behold My hands; and reach here your hand, and thrust it into My side: and be not faithless, but believing." And Thomas answered and said to Him, "My Lord and my God." Jesus said to him, "Thomas, because you have seen Me, you have believed: blessed are they who have not seen, and yet have believed"* (John 20:27-29).

Paul

The other great example that readily comes to mind is our own Apostle, Paul.

Paul (Saul) met the resurrected Jesus Christ on the road to Damascus, and there called Him "Lord" (Acts 9:6). This was all the grand work of God in reaching Paul.

Paul did not believe by simple faith. Rather, it took the dramatic "Damascus Road experience" to bring him to Christ.

During the Dispensation of Grace

Jesus said that Thomas believed by sight. *"Because you have seen Me, you have believed."* Then He goes on to say, *"blessed are they who have **not seen, and yet have believed."***

Those of us today who believe by simple faith are the *Firstfruit* of God's full harvest. We will enjoy the First Resurrection; but this does not exclude the rest of creation, who are awaiting our manifestation:

> *For the earnest expectation of the creature waits for the manifestation of the sons of God* (Romans 8:19).

> *… ourselves also, who have the firstfruits of the Spirit, even we ourselves groan within ourselves, waiting for the adoption, to wit, the redemption of our body* (Romans 8:23).

After the Dispensation of Grace

Both Thomas and Paul met the resurrected Christ! One day, those who have not trusted Christ during this life will be resurrected and brought into the presence of the Son of God, and will with Thomas and Paul call Him "Lord."

Oh, the extent to which God will go to reach man! God is much less limited than Christendom in His evangelism! In due course He can and will pull out all the stops.

> *That at the name of Jesus every knee should bow, of things in heaven, and things in earth, and things under the earth; And that every tongue should confess that Jesus Christ is Lord, to the glory of God the Father* (Philippians 2:10).

Chapter 9

Paul: The Pattern of Salvation for the Unbeliever

This is a faithful saying, and worthy of all acceptation, that Christ Jesus came into the world to save sinners; of whom I am chief. Howbeit for this cause I obtained mercy, that in me first Jesus Christ might show forth all longsuffering, for a pattern to them who should hereafter believe on Him to life everlasting. Now unto the King eternal, immortal, invisible, the only wise God, be honor and glory for ever and ever. Amen. (I Timothy 1:15-17).

Many believers know and understand that Paul is the apostle for this current dispensation, and that he is the source for the knowledge of God's will, His plan and purpose for us today. It is often heard that "Paul is our pattern," and therefore one must experience their salvation in a similar manner as Paul. Yet, is Paul really the *"pattern"* for *our* salvation today? Is this really what I Timothy 1:15-17 is saying?

PAUL'S CONVERSION

Paul was saved in a very different way than we are. His was a salvation by direct divine intervention. Listen in part to Paul give an account of his conversion.

And it came to pass, that, as I made my journey, and came near to Damascus about noon, suddenly there shined from heaven a great light round about me. And I fell unto the ground, and heard a voice saying to me, "Saul, Saul, why are you persecuting Me?" And I answered, "Who are You, Lord? And He said to

me, "I am Jesus of Nazareth, Whom you are persecuting." And
they who were with me saw indeed the light, and were afraid;
but they heard not the voice of Him Who spoke to me ... And
when I could not see for the glory of that light, being led by the
hand of them who were with me, I came into Damascus (Acts
22:6-11).

Damascus Road Experience

Saul did not believe by simple faith (apart from sight). It took the
"Damascus Road experience" to bring him to Christ. He met up
with the resurrected Christ! Oh, the extent to which God will go to
reach man! He is much less limited than we are in His evangelism.

Paul the Pattern of Things to Come

Paul says that his salvation is a pattern for those who should believe
"hereafter," and this salvation shows forth all of God's *"longsuffer-*
ing."

Paul is not only our Apostle in this current age of the Dispensation
of the Grace of God, but he is God's pattern, or type of the salvation
of unbelievers *after their death* (hereafter). The unbelieving, the ob-
stinate, the oppressors, the enemies of God will all have a dramatic
conversion, coming face-to-face with their Savior in the resurrection.

OUR CONVERSION

Considering the above, then, are we saved as Paul was saved? Hardly: Saul, who later was called Paul, was an archenemy of God. It
took the direct hand of God to stop him in his tracks and turn him
around.

When Paul wrote to Timothy he said that his salvation was *"a pat-*
tern" (*i.e.,* a type, a picture); but it was not a pattern of *our* salvation.
Our conversion in no way resembles his.

Blessed Are They Who Have Not Seen, and Yet Have Believed

For those of us who have the privilege of believing now, we are indeed greatly blessed. We are taught this from another account in the Scriptures. It is in the record of "doubting Thomas." Listen to what Thomas, the apostle said.

> *The other disciples therefore said to him* [Thomas], *"We have seen the Lord." But he said to them, "Except I shall see in His hands the print of the nails, and put my finger into the print of the nails, and thrust my hand into His side, I will not believe"* (John 20:25).

Now listen to the response of our Lord Jesus Christ to Thomas.

> *Then He said to Thomas, "Reach your finger here, and behold My hands; and reach your hand hither, and thrust it into My side: and be not faithless, but believing." And Thomas answered and said to Him, "My Lord and my God." Jesus said to him, "Thomas, because you have seen Me, you have believed: blessed are they who have not seen, and yet have believed"* (John 20:27-29).

Jesus said that Thomas believed by sight – *"Because you have seen Me, you have believed."* He goes on to say, *"blessed are they who have not seen, and yet have believed."*

Chapter 10
Faith Given to All

He has given assurance unto all men (Acts 17:31).

The word *"assurance"* here is so translated only twice in the *King James Version* from the Greek word *pistis*,[1] but it is translated 241 times as *"faith."*

Thus, the *Concordant Version* renders it,

Tendering faith to all.

Tyndale translated it,

Faith to all men.

Dabhar renders it,

Having let all have faithing.

God has *"given **faith** unto all men."* That which will be confidently realized in the future is spoken of as being current. After all, He is the God Who *"calls those things which are not as though they were"* (Romans 4:17).

While presently most have not yet been assigned faith, ultimately they will be – and even those who today have been granted faith have been done so only in a *"measure."*

---

1. *Strong's Greek Lexicon #4102, translated "faith."*

According as God has dealt to every man the measure of faith (Romans 12:3).

Currently, divinely-imposed blindness keeps many from embracing the true nature of *"Father."* However, one day this *ignorance* will be completely dispelled by a divinely-given "faith" that will generate genuine *"repentance"* (the thinking of things differently). The result will be,

> *that at the name of Jesus every knee will bow, of things in Heaven, and things in Earth, and things under the Earth; and that every tongue will confess that Jesus Christ is Lord, to the glory of God the Father* (Philippians 2:10-11).

This is not just some kind of optimistic, wishful thinking – but a message of absolute confidence. Paul's message on Mars' Hill faithfully represents the glorious good news given to him for all mankind. His *"my gospel"* concerned the fullness of God's work through His Son, the Lord Jesus Christ.

The Gospel of our Lord and Savior, Jesus Christ, committed to Paul the Apostle, is truly better good news than any of us could ever have imagined! It is far more glorious than any religion would ever have us believe!

God's purpose of the ages will not be completed until His full creative bounty is restored, so that He is *"All IN all"* (I Corinthians 15:28).

I trust that you will be at liberty to set aside religious paradigms and enjoy the amazing riches of Christ's finished work at Calvary!

Chapter 11
Trusting Others to Father

Do you carry the heavy weight of others on your shoulders? That somehow you are responsible for the direction and outcome of their lives?

Being "God" to someone is an especially hard job if you are not qualified. There is only One in the universe qualified for such a daunting task, and He already has all things squarely under His control. So, relax.

God is good at His job. Just like with any other work, you can't judge the finished product when seeing it in some stage of its development. This is true of you and me, of our loved ones and friends – all of God's creation!

When a dinner is being prepared the kitchen may look like a big mess, and the ingredients in their various stages of being mixed, stirred, blended, pounded, chopped, heated, etc. may not taste good or seem as if they will ever amount to anything. It is all just a matter of timing in the kitchen of a master-chef. Just wait until the finished product is taken from the kitchen of preparation and placed on the table of display.

So it is with God and all of His creation. He is still mixing the batter – with all of us. After all, never forget that it was to the idol-worshipping pagans that Paul said,

For in Him we live, and move, and have our being (Acts 17:28).

Don't be depressed as you look around you. What you see is not the end of God's plan and purpose. What you see is not the finished product of God. God is actively at work in us in every circumstance, of every life.

God, Who works *"all things after the counsel of His Own will,"* finds no challenge with the circumstances and lives of our loved ones – not even the hard cases. After all, they are the circumstances of His own making. Nothing poses an obstacle to Him – He is the Almighty God.

God may have chosen you to be one of His instruments of ministry toward your loved ones, but never forget that you are the instrument and not the Master Craftsman. Just as the spoon, the sifter and the whisk are all just tools in the hands of the chef, so it is with you. You are but the utensil in the hands of the Master Chef.

Just as culinary utensils have no life and purpose of their own to create any dish but must be selected and used by the cook – at his own will – so it is with you and me.

Do not be overwhelmed or discouraged: you are not the Workman, but only the utensil in His hand. Whatever comes out of His use of you is completely up to Him.

Relax with those whom God has placed in your life. God is God; He is in charge. He loves them just as unconditionally as He loves you. He is molding them, as surely as He is you – day-by-day – into all that He intends for them to be, regardless of what we may think we currently see.

Do not be tempted to play "God" in the lives of others. Do not be disheartened with His pace, nor with His progress, for He is not yet finished – *but, one day*, you and I and all of our loved ones will finally be completed.

Trust others to the Father.

Chapter 12
Our Response to Blindness

The world is filled with blindness: relatives, friends, neighbors, co-workers. As impairing as physical blindness can be, this is not the one to which I refer. Instead, I speak of one far worse: *spiritual blindness*.

Most go through life groping in the darkness. Only those granted the spiritual eyes to see have any divine light. It is not hard to see the effects of such a condition all around us.

The blinded condition is as divinely ordained as is sight, for,

> *Who appointed a mouth for man, or Who appointed him to be dumb, or seeing, or blind? Is it not I Jehovah?* (Exodus 4:11-12).

Listen as John's Gospel (12:37-40) describes the true condition of unbelief.

> *But though He had done so many miracles before them, yet **they believed not** on Him: that the saying of Isaiah the prophet might be fulfilled, which he spoke,*
>
>> *"Lord, who has believed our report? And to whom has the arm of the Lord been revealed?"*
>
> *Therefore **they could not believe, because** that Isaiah said again,*

*"**He has blinded their eyes,** and hardened their heart;*
***lest they should be seeing** with their eyes, and should be*
understanding with their heart, and be converted."

Those who *"believed not"* simply *"could not believe, because"* God
had *"blinded their eyes," "lest they should be seeing."*

The reason for their blindness is certain; it is divine.

Without the imposition of divine spiritual blindness, all of those of
Jesus' day would have believed. Israel's Messiah *"had done so many
miracles before them,"* it took an act of God to prevent them from
seeing Who He really was.

There is no need to be frustrated or irritated at the divine work of
blindness among our fellow man. Faith will not belittle, make fun
of, or mock them. The blind merely play their part in the divine
drama.

Be careful that we do not fall into a carnal mindset: being demean-
ing, condescending, insulting, disrespectful and sarcastic toward
those who are blind. All such reactions are childish and irrespon-
sible.

Our response toward blindness is compassion, kindness, tender-
heartedness, empathy and graciousness regarding their handicap. It
has been thrust upon them, as equally as has been our sight.

> *For who makes you to be different from another? What do you
> have that you didn't receive? Now, if you received it, why are
> you proud, as if you hadn't received it? (I Corinthians 4:7).*

> *By the grace of God I am what I am: and His grace which was
> bestowed on me was not in vain (I Corinthians 15:10).*

Chapter 11
The Myth of Free Will

I was raised in the "free will" doctrine and taught it diligently for many years as a pastor. We all do have a will: the "problem" is that it isn't free. "Free will" is simply a myth.

We did not choose our race, our nationality, our sex, our eye or hair color, our birth date, or even who our parents were. No "free will" there at all, and that is just for "starters."

"Free-will" is "influenced" by our culture, our society, our peers, our sex, our upbringing, our parents, by our spouses, etc. "Free will" is simply an illusion. Everything about us is a composite of influences around us, in circumstances over which we have no control or choice whatsoever. We did not even choose to be here.

Something as basic as weather conditions restrain our so-called "free will." For instance, we use our "free will" to "choose" to go hiking – then a strong thunderstorm settles in and changes our "free will" plans.

My mother had no "free will" in getting cancer. My father had no "free will" in dying from it. Jenny had no "free will" in her husband abandoning her and her children. Bob had no "free will" in the loss of his job. Jerry had no "free will" in the drunk driver that paralyzed him and killed his son.

Aashish had no "free will" being born, and then living and dying without ever even having heard of the name of the Lord Jesus Christ – not even once, let alone the gospel of what He had done for him.

We all have a "will," but whatever are its characteristics, "free" is definitely not one of them. Even our belief in "free will" is not of our own "choosing" – it was thrust upon mankind by the religious system. It makes for good theology, but it just isn't true. Paul warned us of religion's *"will worship"* (Colossians 2:23); and if we listen closely we can hear this worship of human "free will" in the language of its believers:

"*I* believed in the gospel."

"*I* came to Christ."

"*I* chose to place my faith in Christ."

"*I* decided to live for God."

The disciples may have thought that they chose to follow the Lord, but Jesus set the record straight:

You have not chosen Me, but I have chosen you (John 15:16).

This is why John wrote that the work in Israel was not *"of the will of man, but of God"* (John 1:13).

We all make choices every day, none of which are "free" from some kind of influence. For every effect there is a cause. Ultimately God is behind them all, in them all, and through them all. He *alone* is the great Cause. We, as the clay, cannot also be the Potter. From the human viewpoint man appears to have "free will," but from the divine viewpoint, God,

Works all things after the counsel of His Own will (Ephesians 1:11).

Therefore God's will is free, and man's will is not – it is limited.

Currently all creation is subjected to a temporary "vanity" as a part of God's operation to be All in all.

For the creature was made subject to vanity, not willingly, but by reason of Him Who has subjected the same in hope (Romans 8:20).

Those who do not now believe, just as Paul spoke of Israel, are temporarily *locked up* in unbelief.

God did **SHUT UP** *together the whole to unbelief* (Romans 11:32, *Young's*).

God **LOCKS UP** *all together in stubbornness* (Romans 11:32, *CLNT*).

One day this will all change. For now, God is working in those whom He has chosen; and even His work in us is His Own will and doing.

For it is God Who works in you both to will and to do of His good pleasure (Philippians 2:13).

If God works in the believer to "will," then our will is hardly "free."

As parents we love our children, and they love us "back." They respond to our unconditional love of them. They do not love us out of "free will" – they did not pick us out and "choose" to love us – they were influenced in their "decision" to love us only because we loved them first. They were "set-up!" So it is with God in His relationship with us. We learn this from John's simple words.

We love Him, because He first loved us (I John 4:19).

There is no "free will." The reason that we love Him is completely OUTSIDE of ourselves. His love is the *first cause* from which our love springs. Paul wrote of this love being manifested through the Lord Jesus Christ to us:

> *For the love of Christ constrains us* (II Corinthians 5:14).

His love is not just available, or a potential love, nor an offer of love; but it is a *constraining* love. "Constrain" is a strong word. The Greek word from which it is translated is *sunecho*. James Strong defines it as "to arrest (a prisoner)." The word is so strong that it is used in the Scriptures of being *overtaken* by a disease (Matthew 4:24; Luke 4:38; Acts 28:8).

It is interesting that Paul used this word, for he knew firsthand of Christ's constraining love. It arrested him on the road to Damascus. Paul (Saul) was not seeking Christ. He did not "choose" Him. Paul met the resurrected Jesus Christ on the road to Damascus, and there called Him "Lord" (Acts 9:6). This was all the grand, abrupt, course-altering, sovereign work of God in reaching Paul.

Paul was on his way to Damascus to do harm to the saints there. He did not change his mind by his own "free will." Rather, it was the dramatic "Damascus Road experience" that transformed his will. Paul met with spectacular interference to his "free will." He met the resurrected Christ! One day, those who have not trusted Christ during this life will be resurrected and brought into the presence of the Son of God, and will with Paul call Him "Lord."

> *That at the name of Jesus every knee should bow, of things in heaven, and things in earth, and things under the earth; And that every tongue should confess that Jesus Christ is Lord, to the glory of God the Father* (Philippians 2:10).

Oh, the extent to which God will go to reach man! Isn't it odd how

Christendom limits God's ability, and yet makes man's will free. God is not limited at all, and in due course He will pull out all the stops in reaching mankind with His love.

Paul did not choose to be an Apostle by his "free will," he was "*an Apostle by the WILL OF GOD*" (I Corinthians 1:1; II Corinthians 1:1; Ephesians 1:1; Colossians 1:1; II Timothy 1:1).

There are two "wills" in the universe: the Creator's and the creatures. God's will is FREE, the creatures' is not. God "*will have all men to be saved*" (I Timothy 2:4), and He Who "*works all things after the counsel of His Own will*" (Ephesians 1:11) will "*reconcile all things unto Himself; by Him, I say, whether they be things in earth, or things in heaven*" (Colossians 1:20), making Him "*the Savior of all men*" (I Timothy 4:10).

When my children were young we lived on a busy street with no fence around our house. I would not allow them to play in or near the street. They had no "free will." I constrained them with my love.

We are not the masters of our own fate. We are not the lords of our own lives. We are the creatures, not the Creator. "*He is Lord of ALL*" (Acts 10:36), "*in Him we live, and move, and have our being*" (Acts 17:28), and our response to His love is all a matter of timing, "*but every man in his own order*" (I Corinthians 15:23).

None of us had any "free will" in being included in the disobedience of Adam. It was forced upon us. Neither do any of us have any "free will" about the undoing of Adam in the obedience of Christ.

> *Therefore as by the offence of one* [Adam] *judgment came upon* **ALL MEN** *to condemnation;* **even so** *by the righteousness of One* [Christ] *the free gift came* **UPON ALL** *men unto justification of life* (Romans 5:18).

Not even our faith to believe in Jesus Christ as our Lord and Savior is a matter of our own choosing.

*For by grace are you saved, through faith, and that **not of yourselves:** it is **the gift of God** …* (Ephesians 2:8-9).

THIS is the good news, believe it or not.

If we believe not, yet He abides faithful: He cannot deny Himself (II Timothy 2:13).

Chapter 12

God's <u>Free</u> Will and Man's <u>Limited</u> Will

When we speak negatively of humanity's *free* will we do not suggest that we don't have a will at all. We have a will, it is just not *free*;[1] neither do we have the unrestricted ability to carry out our will.

God, on the other hand has a will that is absolutely *free*,[2] and without any restriction in executing it whatsoever. In other words, His will is absolutely *sovereign*[3] without restraint from any outside source.

What is thus the current practical purpose, beyond God's own sovereignty, for humanity's will being limited?

God is the Father and we are His children. Relatively speaking, when my children were young they had a will, but it was not free. I caused the exercise of their will to be *limited*, while mine in relationship to theirs was *sovereign*. So it is with God.

To advocate human free will is to deny God's Godhood. For there to be a God, there can't be two conflicting wills. There is room in

---

1. "Not limited" – *Cambridge*; "unconstrained; unrestrained; not under compulsion or control … not obstructed" – *Webster* (1828).
2. Interestingly, "free" is a synonym of "sovereign."
3. "Self-governing; independent … having supreme rank or power …" – *American Heritage Dictionary*.

His universe for only one with free will. It is impossible for a finite being to have an absolutely free will. If creatures had absolute free will, then the creation would be greater than the Creator. God's will is FREE; man's will is NOT.

Based on fancied "free will," Christianity essentially has God gambling on an experiment. We, however, are not the masters of our own fate. We are not the lords of our own lives. We are the creatures, not the Creator. We are like a leaf in a stream, unaware of the current beneath, or its destination.

We can relax in our constrained wills as creatures, and rest in Father's free will as Creator. He is our benevolent Dad; He always knows exactly what He is doing, and those of us granted faith have the eyes to see that it all works for eventual good.

Chapter 13

The Effect of Faith on Unbelieving Spouses and Children

The unbelieving husband is hallowed by the wife, and the unbelieving wife is hallowed by the brother, else, consequently, your children are unclean. Yet now they are holy (I Corinthians 7:14).

I often think about the effect of faith on those around us. While I used to be critical of what I referred to as "secondhand faith," I do see the value that others can obtain by being around those who have been granted faith by God.

For not one of us is living to himself, and not one is dying to himself (Romans 14:7, CV).

Faith has a divine influence, not only on its recipient, but also on those whose lives interact with them. The effect of faith can leave its mark on the unbelieving as well.

Paul clearly teaches that one such profound effect of faith is on the spouses and children of believers.

*The unbelieving husband is **hallowed** by the wife, and the unbelieving wife is **hallowed** by the brother, else, consequently, your children are unclean. Yet now they are **holy*** (I Corinthians 7:14).

According to Paul, unbelieving spouses and children become associated with an important part of their election: they are declared *"sanctified"* and *"holy."* Such is said by Scripture to be the divine impact of faith on them.

We will make note of two Greek words used by Paul in I Corinthians 7:14. The first is ἁγιάζω (*hagiazō*),[1] and the other is its root word ἅγιος (*hagios*).[2] *Hagiazō* appears twice in the verse, both times rendered as "*sanctified*" in the *KJV* and *YLT* – and "*hallowed*" in *CV*, *RE* and *DT*. *Hagios* is found once, translated "*holy.*"

Under Israel's prior economy, various things, places, and grounds were said to be "*sanctified,*" or "*hallowed,*" and thus "*holy.*" Interestingly, in relationship to people we see *hagios* translated "*saints.*" Accordingly, a consistent, concordant translation would render the last phrase of the verse as,

> *Yet now they are* **saints.**

This is quite profound language coming from the pen of Paul, for he is also plain in his declaration that there is surely an allotment to be enjoyed "*among* **all** *who have been hallowed* [*hagiazō*]" (Acts 20:32). If words mean anything, especially those of the original language, then unbelieving spouses and children are among the "*all*" who will be enjoying future allotments, right alongside their believing counterparts. Such is the powerful effect of faith upon these closest of human relationships.

It's important for us to proclaim *exactly* what the Scriptures declare. Equally true, we must not assert what they do not affirm. While unbelieving spouses are *hagiazō* ("*hallowed*"), and thus *hagios* ("*saints*"), they are nonetheless not presently said to be "*believers,*" members of the "*ecclesia which is His Body,*" "*elect,*" etc.

Yet not to worry: for just as the allotment of Israel's election gained an effect for those (such as servants) to whom it was not directly allotted, likewise, despite unbelieving spouses and children having no *title* to the allotment, they nonetheless will share in its *enjoyment*.

A modern example may well serve as a suitable illustration. Those who obtain an *election* to the Presidency of the United States receive

---

1. *SEC*, G37.
2. *SEC*, G40.

a specific position and allotment of ascendency. They are *chosen* to a place of authority (*e.g.* Commander-in-Chief) and to a place of dwelling (The White House). Although it is only those who were *chosen by election* who have any rights to this important role of service, they do *not* travel to Washington D.C. alone. They bring those of their household with them. Though these spouses and children have no election, choosing, calling or official position, they nevertheless enjoy the grand effect of the allotment of 1600 Pennsylvania Avenue just the same.

Likewise it is with the spouses and children of I Corinthians 7:14. So great is the divine impact of faith!

סֶלָה *Selâh.*[3]

---

3. *SEC*, H5542. Selâh appears 74 times in the Hebrew Scriptures – 71 in the Psalms and 3 in Habakkuk.

    It means to "be silent, to pause a little" ... "Primarily, indeed, it is a music mark, but it generally appears where a pause is suitable. The right view of this word was substantially given by Luther. The selah, says he, tells us "to pause and carefully reflect on the words" (Hengstenberg). – William Wilson (1783-1873), *Old Testament Word Studies*

    Or, as Dr. Bud Lyles (1928-2018) would say, "Selah: Well, think of that!"

Your Part

Now that you have read this book, it's your turn.

If the truths presented here have helped you, don't let these truths die in your hands.

Please write to us and let us know your thoughts concerning its content.

Consider assisting us in getting this book into the hands of those who would be encouraged and strengthened by its message:

- Recommend it to your friends and loved ones.

- Order additional copies to give as gifts.

- Keep extra copies on hand to loan to others.

If you have not read the author's other works, order them today.

We would be honored to have your fellowship in getting this book freely to those who hunger spiritually. We have daily opportunities to send it to pastors, Sunday school teachers, Bible college professors and students, Bible class teachers, and prisoners.

CLYDE L. PILKINGTON, JR.

Another Look at "Bible Study" – The Misuse of II Timothy 2:15 and the Abuse of Christ's Body

"You continue to bless me with messages that relieve the burden." – *Illinois*

"Helped me shed major bondage." – *Michigan*

"What a freeing teaching." – *Pennsylvania*

"Finally relieved me of yet another religious burden." – *Poland*

"Such a balm to my soul." – *Canada*

(#0370) 65 pages, paperback, *$4.*^{95}

Being OK with Not Being OK: Embracing God's Design for You – and Everyone You Know (and Don't Know)

For now, you're broken, and you aren't going to be "fixed." Granted, you may have some days that are better than others, some circumstances that seem to indicate that you are "OK," but the wearisome cycle simply will recur.

Thus it is by design – by divine design. Father is bringing you to a place where you are OK with not being OK, where you simply rest in His current purpose and plan in your training and development for that grand and magnificent culmination that He has so wonderfully and skillfully designed especially for you – in your next life. 134 pages, paperback.

#1985 Single copy *$9.*^{95}

#1986 5-pack (*$7.*^{50} each) *$37.*^{50}

#1987 10-pack (*5.*^{95} each) *$59.*^{50}

The Believer's Warfare: Wearing the Armor of Light in the Darkness of this World

(#7000) The believer is in the middle of an ancient spiritual warfare that is as old as mankind. The battle itself, although intense, is not complicated. It is not a process of spiritual hoop-jumping. Indeed it is simple. The Believer's Warfare surveys a few key passages of Scripture to reveal God's sure plan of victory in the life of His saints. 84 pages, paperback. *$9.*^{95}

The Bible Student's Notebook (VOLUMES)

The *Bible Student's Notebook* is a periodical dedicated to the: – Promotion of Bible study – Encouragement of the believer's growth in grace – Support of the role of family patriarch – Recovery of truth that has too long been hidden under the veils of traditionalism, prejudice, misunderstanding and fear. The Bible Student's Notebook is not connected with any "Church," "Movement," "Organization," "Society," "Mission," or separate body of believers, but is sent forth to and for all of God's saints. Available in paperback Volumes. *$19.*^{95} ea. (current BSN

Master Index $5.^{25}). For individual volumes, see listing under Periodicals. For individual volumes, see listing under Periodicals.

The Church in Ruins: Brief Thoughts on II Timothy

(#3325) This brief survey of Paul's last epistle will reveal that while almost 2000 years have transpired, the condition of the church has remained the same, and indeed has worsened in accordance with Paul's warning to Timothy. This book is not a call for a re-awakening of "the church," because it is apparent that this is not Father's plan. Rather, it is a call to individual men – men whose place in the Christian religious system has left them empty, stagnant, and restless – to awaken to Father's call to be His faithful servant and stand outside of that system to look for other faithful men as well. 128 pages, paperback.

#3325 Single copy *$9.$^{25}*
#3326 5-pack (*$7.$^{50}* each) *$37.$^{50}*
#3327 10-pack (*$5.$^{25}* each) *$59.$^{50}*
#5050 Combo, w/The Outsiders *$14.$^{25}*

Daily Gleanings – 365 Selections on Scriptural Truths

(#1836) This book contains a collection of gleanings from some 200 different authors. These excerpts are intended to be an encouragement to those who are walking on a different path with the Lord – a journey that is *"outside of the camp."*

Some quotations are from beloved and trusted authors, but more often than not, they are from unusual sources. Sometimes, it is simply amazing how an author can admit in print to some grand truth that their writings and ministries otherwise generally deny. For the authors of these quotes, the truth that is conveyed by them may oddly seem "out of place"; but in some ways, the more unlikely the source, the more amazingly it testifies to the truth – and the fact that it cannot be hidden. 253 pages, paperback. *$19.$^{95}*

Daily Goodies: 365 Thoughts on Scriptural Truths

(#1747) This is a great resource for personal and family study, as well as a valuable reference volume covering many varied biblical themes. This is a collection of choice selections from the author's Daily E-mail Goodies. These free daily e-mails began being issued in 2003 and contain studies on scriptural themes. 490 pages, paperback. *$19.$^{95}*

Divine Lockup

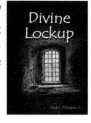

(#0554) This work deals scripturally with God's sovereignty in the midst of humanity's current condition of, and future deliverance from, unbelief, sin, vanity and corruption. Without question, for all creation, the best is yet to come. 66 pages, paperback. *$9.$^{25}*

#0554 Single copy *$9.$^{25}*
#0555 5-pack (*$7.$^{50}* each) *$37.$^{50}*
#0556 10-pack (*$5.$^{25}* each) *$59.$^{50}*

Due Benevolence: A Study of Biblical Sexuality

(#3775) Think you have read all that there is on the subject of sexuality from the Bible? Think again! Religious moralists have taken the wonderful gift of human beauty and sexuality and made it something dirty and sinful. Much is at stake regarding truth, as well as the nature and character of God Himself. A groundbreaking work providing ...

• A refreshingly honest and uninhibited look at sexuality.
• A breath of fresh air from the religious and Victorian mentality.
• A daring and valuable glimpse at the wonderful light just outside sexuality's prison-cell door.

220 pages, paperback. *$19.*^{25}

God 101: Back to Basics

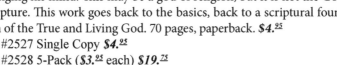

(#2527) Sadly, there are some who would teach of a god who somehow does not know all things, is not all powerful, is not sovereign, and is always changing his mind. This may be a god of religion, but it is not the God of Scripture. This work goes back to the basics, back to a scriptural foundation of the True and Living God. 70 pages, paperback. *$4.*^{25}

#2527 Single Copy *$4.*^{25}
#2528 5-Pack (*$3.*^{25} each) *$19.*^{75}
#2529 10-Pack (*$2.*^{25} each) *$29.*^{50}

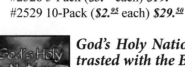

God's Holy Nation: Israel and Her Earthly Purpose (Contrasted with the Body of Christ and Its Heavenly Purpose)

(#2275) Israel plays a key role in God's plan of the ages. Though currently she has been set aside "until the times of the nations be fulfilled," He is by no means done with her.

Today, God is operating His purpose in the ecclesia – the Church, the Body of Christ. The Scriptures provide us with the clear, critical distinction between God's earthly nation and Christ's celestial body.

Christendom, however, has diminished Israel's divine significance in an attempt to advance their artificial homogenization of Scripture's grand theme, thus obscuring the glorious evangel of our day – "the Good News of the Happy God" committed to the trust of Paul, our Apostle.

This work highlights some of the more prominent distinctions which belong to God's literal, physical, earthly nation. In so doing, it is our desire to allow the reader to see more clearly God's dealings with God's favored nation, so that they may in turn embrace a far greater calling and purpose. 360 pages, paperback. *$19.*^{25}

The Great Omission: Christendom's Abandonment of the Biblical Family

(#2010) This book presents twenty years of study, taking a candid look at the issue of multiple wives in Scripture and society. The book chapters are: The Problem; The Divine Provision; The Marital Gift; The Old Testament Scriptural Precedent; The New Testament Scriptural Precedent; The Religious System's Destruction of the Biblical Family; The History of Its Practice; The Cultural Issue. This book also has 14 appendixes. 204 pages, paperback.

#2010 Single copy *$14.^{95}*
#2011 5-pack (*$10* each) *$50*
#2012 10-pack (*$8.^{75} each) $87.^{50}*

Heaven's Embassy: The Divine Plan & Purpose of the Home

(#5675) The home is central to all of God's dealings with man throughout the course of time. It is His Divine "institution" and "organization" on the earth; and for the believer, it is the Embassy of Heaven. An embassy is "the residence or office of an ambassador." Since the believer is an ambassador of the Lord Jesus Christ (II Corinthians 5:14-21), his home is thus the Divine Embassy of heavenly ministry. Pauline ministry is centered in the homes of believers. This is even the true sphere of the Body of Christ; for this reason our apostle speaks of "church in thy house." This book doesn't focus upon the external specifics of the ministry of Heaven's Embassy (such as hospitality); that will be saved for another volume. Instead, it looks at the inner-workings of the Embassy itself; focusing upon its very nature and internal purpose and function. 250 pages, paperback. *$19.^{95}*

I Am! Who and What God Says I Am! The Divine Reckoning of the Renewed Mind; Daily Thoughts on Divine Life

(#1737) People are always talking about their attempts to discover their true selves – of trying to "find themselves." The believer in the Lord Jesus Christ needs to find out who they *really* are. This doesn't need to be such a difficult search. All that is really needed is a careful look at the Scriptures, and a simple faith in the words of who and what God says we are. God knows who we are; all we need to do is to *believe Him*. This book catalogs the Divine Record of who and what God says that you are. It is a short encyclopedia of faith – the truth about you. It is the truth about you, simply because it is *God* Who has said it. God has spoken these truths concerning you – the *real* you. Believe His record! Refuse to be the shell of a person, pushed into a mold of Adamic conformity. Be the real you that God has uniquely designed you to be. Refuse to be bullied out of your divinely designed identity that our Father has given you. 107 pages, paperback. *$9.^{95}*

#1737 (Single Copy) *$9.^{95}*
#1738 5-Pack (*$7.^{50} each) $37.^{50}*
#1739 10-Pack (*$5.^{95} each) $59.^{95}*
#1740 20-Pack (*$4.^{50} each) $90*

I Choose! Living Life to Its Fullest

(#4120) Forty-Eight Daily Thoughts on Divine Life. You are alive! Yet not just alive, but alive with the very life of God! Don't allow your "What if …" imaginations of the past or the future to lay claim to the present that God has given you. Allow the objective, unchanging truth of who God has made you in the Lord Jesus Christ to transform your mind and life as you take this spiritual journey of "I Choose." These "choices" are not to be confused with so-called "free will." At the close of the book the author will reveal that our "choices" are nothing short of God's sovereign decree in our lives. 192 pages, paperback. *$16.^{25}*

King James Version, The – 400 Years of Bondage – 1611-2011

(#4682) 1611 was not a high spiritual mark in the history of the church, the Body of Christ. Instead of being a grand year of the pinnacle of preservation or perfection of God's Word, it was rather the sad depths of the subtle corrupting of God's Word by the historic union of governmental and ecclesiastical politics. 72 pages, paperback. *$9.^{25}*

A Look at Alcohol in the Scriptures

(#1150) Wine was a blessing in Scripture (Proverbs 3:10), something to be received gratefully from God (Psalm 104:15). Like many things that God has graciously given to man, alcohol can be used or abused.

However it is important that we do not confuse use with abuse, or drinking with drunkenness. To prohibit the use of alcohol, by pointing to verses about its abuse, would be like condemning the eating of food because of gluttony, or requiring sexual abstinence because of carnal sins. This is deceptive and erroneous religious reasoning.

This study briefly surveys alcohol related Hebrew and Greek words and some of their contexts, considers passages usually used to condemn the use of alcohol, and looks at a few common objections. 54 pages, paperback, *$5.^{25}*

The Myth of Easter

(#1675) There are many myths in Christendom. They have managed to master their own form of mythology. Easter is an example of such a religious fable.

If Easter is the celebration of the historical fact of our Lord Jesus Christ's resurrection, then why does its date change every year? Historical dates do not fluctuate; but Easter Sunday can fall anywhere between March 22 and April 25. Have you ever wondered why?

It is one of the glaring clues that something is seriously wrong with Christendom. The Western Christian religion can't seem to get anything right when it comes to even the simplest of Scriptural truths.

Have you ever really considered if there is any scriptural basis of Good Friday or Easter Sunrise Services that are so commonly observed by the religious community? Additionally, have you ever considered what Easter Rabbits and Easter Eggs have to do with the resurrection of Christ or teachings of God's Word?

Although millions of people are of the opinion that Easter and all of its customs are Christian and originated as a result of Christ's resurrection, it is a historical fact that the observance of Easter long antedates Christianity by centuries. 72 pages, Booklet, *$4.$*^{95}

Nothing Will Be Lost! The Truth About God's Good News

(#3750) This is an abridgement of the larger work *The Salvation of All*. It is designed as a give-away edition, with quantity pricing available. 88 pages, paperback. *$9.$*^{95}

#3750 Single copy *$9.$*^{95}
#3752 5-pack (*$7.$*^{50} each) *$37.$*^{50}
#3751 10-pack (*$5.$*^{95} each) *$59.$*^{50}

The Outsiders: God's Called-Out Ones – A Biblical Look at the Church – God's Ecclesia

(#4125) In 1995, after sixteen years of being in the "pastorate" the author walked away. He left the "religious system" by resigning from the very "church" and "ministry" he had formed. In many ways this work is a testament to these actions. This testimony was thirty years in the making -- the results of a spiritual journey that the author found to be common to other saints scattered throughout the world and across history. This is an opportunity to explain why some who love the Lord no longer "go to church." It does not seek to persuade others to do something different; but rather to simply be who and what they already are "in Him." This is an uncovering of the truth of the church, and an encouragement for the members of His Body to enjoy the position and standing "in Christ" that they already possess, realizing that they are truly "complete in Him" (Colossians 2:10), that He alone is their Life (Colossians 3:4), and that His Life is full of freedom (Galatians 5:1). 128 pages, paperback. *$9.$*^{95}

#4125 Single copy *$9.$*^{95}
#4126 5-pack (*$7.$*^{50} each) *$37.$*^{50}
#4127 10-pack (*$5.$*^{95} each) *$59.$*^{50}
#5050 Combo, w/The Outsiders *$14.$*^{95}

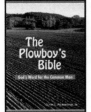

The Plowboy's Bible: God's Word for Common Man

(#4425) Shocking conclusions from the man that brought you The King James Bible Song. This book represents years of study and a significant change in understanding. Raised on and trained in a "King James Only" position, most of the author's teaching ministry was centered on the defense of the KJV. He had early associations with major proponents of this position and their followers. He actively taught classes and seminars on the subject of Bible versions. For many years he distributed thousands of books from a collection of over 100 different titles in support of the KJV position. Here he shares what he has come to see that has caused him to completely abandon his former position. 254 pages, paperback. *$19.$*^{95}

The Salvation of ALL: Creation's Final Destination (A Biblical Look at Universal Reconciliation)

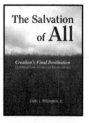

(#7001) The Gospel of our Lord and Savior, Jesus Christ is truly better "Good News" than we could ever have imagined. It is far more glorious than religion would ever have us believe. *The Salvation of All* is a book about a "Good News" that will reach its final goal in the salvation of all mankind. 262 pages, paperback. *$19.*^{95}

The Steps I Have Taken – A Short Auto-biographical Work

(#1175) Many times over the years Clyde has been asked how he got from an Independent Baptist pastor to where he is now: from a hell-fire and brimstone street preacher to a herald of the good news of "the happy God." This work is a short chronicle of his journey: leaving the confines of religious bondage to enjoying the life of God in the wide open spaces of His grace. 65 pages, paperback, *$5.*^{95}

Suffering: God's Forgotten Gift

(#5150)Two gifts given to the believer are mentioned by Paul in Philippians 1:29. The first is "to believe on Him." This is a glorious gift. Every believer has been given this gift from God. Those who possess it may not even fully recognize it as a gift from Him, but indeed faith is God's wonderful gift to us. Faith is a rich gift from God, but there is also another gift from God to the believer, mentioned by Paul in Philippians 1:29, that is equally as glorious. The second gift is "also to suffer for His sake." This, too, is a glorious gift. Every believer has been given this gift from God as well, but those who possess it often do not fully recognize it for what it is. Indeed, suffering for His sake similarly is God's wonderful gift to us. Paul teaches us to embrace this second gift as well as we do the first! 100 pages, paperback. *$9.*^{95}

    #5150 Single copy *$9.*^{95}
    #5152 5-pack (*$7.*^{50} each) *$37.*^{50}
    #5151 10-pack (*$5.*^{95} each) *$59.*^{50}

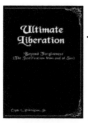

Ultimate Liberation: Beyond Forgiveness (The Justification from and of Sin)

(#2510) Many people labor under a heavy weight of guilt and shame. The answer is to be found only in the total provision that God Himself has already provided! 60 pages, paperback, *$4.*^{95}

    #2510 (Single Copy) *$4.*^{95}
    #2511 (5-Pack/*$3.*^{95} each) *$19.*^{75}
    #2512 (10-Pack/*$2.*^{95} each) *$29.*^{50}

The Undoing of Adam and the Approach Present of God

(#5313) Christ is greater than Adam, undoing what Adam did. In fact, Christ's work at Calvary is greater than Adam's fall. All of God's creation will be gloriously saved by the successful work of "*the Savior of the world*" (John 4:42). Salvation is not dependent on us at all; it is all about Christ and His work alone. Paul taught that the exact same "*all*" who are condemned in Adam are the exact same "*all*" who are justified in Christ (Romans 5:18), and that the exact same "*all*" who die in Adam are the exact same "*all*" who are "*made alive*" in Christ (I Corinthians 15:22). Christianity has an Adam who is greater than Christ; however, it is Christ Who is greater than Adam.

A note concerning the cover: We wanted a cover that would immediately convey the theme of the book's content, choosing to go with a traditional "cross" scene to express the work of Christ at Calvary. Yet Christ did not die on a "cross," but was nailed to a simple "stake." An explanation is provided in the appendix. 98 pages, paperback. *$10.*$^{\underline{95}}$

> #5313 Single copy *$9.*$^{\underline{95}}$
> #5310 5-pack (*$7.*$^{\underline{50}}$ each) *$37.*$^{\underline{50}}$
> #5311 10-pack (*$5.*$^{\underline{25}}$ each) *$59.*$^{\underline{50}}$
> #5312 20-pack (*$4.*$^{\underline{50}}$ each) *$90*

Wife Loving: The Husband's Paramount Privilege

(#0462) This book is about Christ-mentored husbandry; a look at husbands' important and honored role of loving their wives. So lofty and divine is its pursuit, Paul presents none other than Christ Himself as the mentor: "*Husbands, love your wives, even as Christ also loved the church.*" 185 pages, paperback. *$9.*$^{\underline{95}}$

"Powerful, powerful stuff! As a woman I am honored by it. I am deeply grateful for your boldness to honor women and to portray the marriage relationship as simply yet profoundly as God intended." – *CA*

"What wonderful thoughts. They are so true and practical. I love it!" – *The Netherlands*

"I have seldom read so much wisdom on marriage in relation to biblical principles." – *Denmark*

World Affairs and National Politics – and the High Calling of God in Christ Jesus

(#4250) When did nationalism begin? What is God's purpose for nationalism? Is the United States a Christian nation? Does any government have Favored Nation Status with God today? Should believers support Israel? What did Paul have to say about our citizenship? What is our role in relation to nations? Is our job to rid the world of evil? What should the believer's attitude be toward earthly authority? Should all obedience to earthly magistrates be absolute? Are believers to pay their taxes? Where does voting and jury duty fit in? Why was the apostle Paul executed? These and many other questions are addressed in this groundbreaking work! 258 pages, paperback. *$14.^{95}*

TO ORDER:

visit: www.ClydePilkington.com

or

call Toll Free: 1-800-784-6010

Do You Subscribe to the
Bible Student's Notebook™ ?

This is a periodical that ...

- Promotes the study of the Bible.
- Encourages the growth of the believer in grace.
- Supports the role of the family patriarch.
- Is dedicated to the recovery of truth that has too long been hidden under the veils of traditionalism, prejudice, misunderstanding and fear.
- Is not connected with any "Movement," "Organization," "Mission," or separate body of believers, but is sent forth to and for all saints.

The *Bible Student's Notebook*™ is a *free* electronic publication published semi-weekly (100 times a year).

SUBSCRIBE TODAY!

To receive your *free* electronic subscription, email us at:
bsn@studyshelf.com

Bible Student's Notebook™
PO Box 265 Windber, PA 15963
www.BibleStudentsNotebook.com
1-800-784-6010

DAILY EMAIL
GOODIES™

Do you receive our
Daily Email Goodies™?

These are free daily emails that contain short quotes, articles, and studies on Biblical themes.

These are the original writings of Clyde L. Pilkington, Jr, as well as gleanings from other authors.

<u>Here is what our readers are saying</u>:

"Profound! Comforting! Calming! Wonderful!" – NC

"The Daily Email Goodies continue to bless my heart! ... They provide plenty of food for thought." – IL

"I really appreciate the Goodies!" – VA

"Your Daily Email Goodies are making me aware of authors whose names I don't even know." – GA

"I am glad to be getting the Daily Email Goodies – keep 'em coming." – IN

Request to be added to our free
Daily Email Goodies™

If you would like to be added to the mailing list, email us at:

Goodies@StudyShelf.com

ENJOY BOOKS?

Visit us at:

www.StudyShelf.com

Over the years we have often been asked to recommend books. The requests come from believers who longed for material with substance. Study Shelf™ is a collection of books which are, in our opinion, the very best in print. Many of these books are "unknown" to the members of the Body of Christ at large, and most are not available at your local "Christian" bookstore.

YOU CAN:

Read

A wealth of articles from past issues of the *Bible Student's Notebook* ™

Purchase

Rare and hard to find books, booklets, leaflets, Bibles, etc. in our 24/7 online store.